Accounting for Homeowners' Associations

Steven M. Bragg

AccountingTools®

ISBN-13: 978-1-64221-145-0

For more information about AccountingTools® products, visit our Web site at www.ac-countingtools.com.

Table of Contents

About the Author

Steven Bragg, CPA, has been the chief financial officer or controller of four companies, as well as a consulting manager at Ernst & Young. He received a master's degree in finance from Bentley College, an MBA from Babson College, and a Bachelor's degree in Economics from the University of Maine. He has been a two-time president of the Colorado Mountain Club, and is an avid alpine skier, mountain biker, and certified master diver. Mr. Bragg resides in Centennial, Colorado. He has written more than 300 books and courses, including *New Controller Guidebook*, *GAAP Guidebook*, and *Payroll Management*. He has also written *The Auditors* science fiction trilogy.

Steven maintains the accountingtools.com web site, which contains continuing professional education courses, the Accounting Best Practices podcast, and thousands of articles on accounting subjects.

Buy Additional AccountingTools Courses

AccountingTools offers more than 1,500 hours of CPE courses, with concentrations in accounting, auditing, finance, taxation, and ethics. Related courses that you might like include:

- Property Management Accounting
- Property Management Best Practices
- Real Estate Accounting
- Real Estate Tax Guide

Go to accountingtools.com/cpe to view these additional courses.

AccountingTools®

Accounting for Homeowners' Associations

Introduction

This course covers all aspects of the accounting for a homeowners' association. In addition, it covers the accounting for all types of common interest realty associations, which means that it also covers condominium associations, cooperative housing corporations, and time-share associations. After the introductory topics, the general flow of the course is the accounting for assets, liabilities, equity, revenue, expenses, and then financial reporting – with a few additional topics included in the mix.

Common Interest Realty Associations

A *common interest realty association* (CIRA) is an association of owners that is responsible for the provision of services and the maintenance of property that is shared by or owned in common by the owners (generally referred to in this course as residents). They may also provide other services to their members, such as trash removal services and local security. A CIRA may also have to engage in some enforcement activities, such as architectural restrictions and local compliance with state and local statutes. On top of those activities, it must assess fees and collect them from members, in order to have sufficient funds to pay for its own expenses. A CIRA's characteristics will vary to some extent, depending on the type of real estate of which it is comprised.

Examples of this type of association are:

- *Condominium association.* An arrangement in which all unit owners own the interiors of their living spaces, as well as an undivided percentage interest in any common property – for which they have an obligation to pay a pro rata share of the expenses. The common areas include the structure of the building, including its exterior and common walls, roof, plumbing and electrical, and foundation.
- *Cooperative housing corporation (a coop).* An arrangement in which the residents own shares in the coop, giving them the right to own a unit within the building under a proprietary leasing arrangement. The coop owns all real estate within the development, including the individual units. The coop as a whole is responsible for any debt associated with the real estate, and is directly assessed property taxes based on the total value of the overall property. The coop issues monthly assessments to its residents to pay for their share of the organization's costs. This means that residents are not directly liable to creditors of the coop. However, if a resident does not pay his or her obligations to the coop, the other tenants will have to make up the difference in order to keep the coop from defaulting on its payments. Given this level of financial interdependence, the coop's board of directors usually has to approve unit transfers to a new resident, thereby ensuring that new resident have sufficient financial resources.

- *Homeowners' association (HOA)*. An arrangement in which the residents all own a home and the land on which it sits, while the HOA owns all common property. These associations are usually formed within communities of single-family homes or multi-unit buildings, such as townhomes or condominiums. Those who purchase property within an HOA's jurisdiction automatically become members and are required to pay dues, which are known as HOA fees.
- *Time-share association*. An arrangement in which users can occupy a unit within a class of accommodations, typically in weekly increments. Depending on the arrangement, residents may buy the right to use vacation property, but receive no rights in the real estate. Or, they may acquire both the right of usage and an interest in the accommodation. When the arrangement is a right-of-use only, a CIRA is typically not created. Instead, the time-share association takes over the functions normally taken on by a CIRA.

There are a few variations on the concept that may not result in the formation of a CIRA. For example:

- *Condominium hotels*. An arrangement in which buyers own a unit in a hotel for a certain number of weeks per year. The unit is rented out as a hotel room the rest of the time.
- *Master association*. An arrangement in which several CIRAs share common facilities (usually recreational, such as tennis courts or a pool). The participating CIRAs are responsible for maintaining these facilities, which includes assessments to pay for them.
- *Townhouse*. An arrangement in which the property owners own their residences, while sharing a common wall and possibly other common property.

In addition, residents may ask a CIRA to form a subsidiary corporation to conduct activities in which they want to engage, but which are separate from the primary activities of the CIRA. For example, a CIRA could form a corporation to run a golf ship, restaurant, or equestrian center.

The CIRA type of ownership situation typically has the following characteristics:

- Residents own specific lots or interior spaces, or own shares of stock in a property
- Residents have an undivided interest in common property
- Residents are automatically assigned ownership in an association that maintains property and provides services
- Residents are bound by restrictive covenants that are enforced by the CIRA
- Residents are assessed an amount at intervals to fund the association

Common Property

We have already made several references to common property. This is comprised of all property within a CIRA, not including the property owned by the residents living in the development. Thus, common property can include both property directly owned by the CIRA and property owned by the residents in common. Examples of common property are buildings, recreational areas, landscaped areas, parking lots, swimming pools, clubhouses, courtyards, and roads. In addition, the common property for cooperatives and condominiums may include exterior and common walls, roofs, land, plumbing, and electrical.

The Need for CIRA Accounting

At the root of all CIRA accounting is the need to issue annual financial reports to the various property owners. Also, depending on the applicable state laws, these financial reports may need to be audited, reviewed or compiled by a CPA. Furthermore, these reports must be issued to the owners within a range of two to four months of year-end.

Who Conducts CIRA Accounting?

In many cases, and especially with smaller organizations, the governing body of a CIRA will hire a managing agent. This party is responsible for maintaining the accounting records, as well as for billing residents, collecting assessments, overseeing maintenance, and preparing financial statements. Alternatively, the governing body may split these functions and give the bookkeeping activities to a different outside group, or employ its own accounting staff.

With the preliminaries out of the way, we will commence with the accounting for CIRA assets, beginning with the accounting for cash.

Accounting for CIRA Cash

A CIRA receives substantial amounts of cash from its residents, but a large part of it will likely be set aside for specific purposes, which triggers certain accounting and disclosure requirements, as discussed next. There are also disclosures related to where the funds are temporarily invested prior to their use.

Cash Set Aside for a Specific Purpose

The accounting for cash by a CIRA does not vary from standard practice. However, the amount of cash on hand can be substantial, because of the reserves held for future repairs and asset replacements. In particular, this cash is set aside for a specific purpose, and so is not available for general operating activities. Instead, it should be disclosed as having been restricted for a specific use. If the use for which it is intended is more than 12 months in the future, then this cash should be classified as a long-term asset on the balance sheet.

A CIRA may set aside cash for other reasons. For example, it could collect funds on behalf of a holiday party committee, to be disbursed for the event. Or, it may require tenants to pay a deposit when they are given facility keys, which will be returned when they eventually sell their units. These transactions are typically recorded in separate accounts, to facilitate ease of tracking.

Disclosure of Invested Cash

If cash has been parked in an investment vehicle that has a withdrawal restriction, then it generally should be classified as an investment. This does not have much of an impact on the entity's balance sheet, but will shift the reported investment to the investing activities section of the statement of cash flows.

Disclosure of Restricted Cash

If cash has been legally restricted, it is probably designated as a reserve that will be used to pay for a specific liability, such as a debt. If so, it should be classified on the balance sheet as having a duration that matches that of the associated liability. Thus, when cash is restricted to pay for a long-term debt, the cash should also be classified as a long-term asset.

Disclosure of Uninsured Cash

A CIRA may have a substantial amount of cash on hand, especially when it has a replacement fund. If so, it is likely to have been invested in a relatively short-term fund where some of the funds are not covered by insurance. If so, the accountant should disclose this issue in the financial statements as a concentration of credit risk.

Accounting for Marketable Securities

A CIRA may invest its excess cash in marketable securities, which are easily traded investments that are readily convertible into cash, usually because there is a strong secondary market for them. A CIRA may invest in debt securities, such as U.S. Treasury bills, in order to avoid the valuation swings that can occur with equity securities. When acquired, these debt securities may be classified in one of three ways, which are as follows:

- *Held to maturity.* These are debt securities for which the CIRA has the intent and ability to hold all the way to maturity. This classification is unlikely, especially when the CIRA is not sure how long it will hold the security. Record these investments at their amortized cost.
- *Trading security.* These are securities that the CIRA does not intend to hold to maturity; instead, they are expected to be sold in the near term. Measure these securities at their fair value on the balance sheet, and include all unrealized holding gains and losses in earnings.
- *Available for sale.* These are securities that do not fall into either of the preceding categories. This is the most common designation used by CIRAs.

4

Measure these securities at their fair value on the balance sheet, and include all unrealized holding gains and losses in *other comprehensive income* until realized (i.e., when the securities are sold).

The CIRA accountant will also need to periodically evaluate whether the carrying amounts of any of these securities have become impaired, and write them down if this is the case.

In the less-common cases in which excess funds are invested in equity securities, the CIRA is to record them at their fair value through net income.

Accounting for Receivables

The accounting for receivables is centered on the billing and receipt of assessments to residents. This is handled through the CIRA accounting software, and should present no particular issues for the accountant. The main issue is to verify in advance that the assessments being apportioned to each resident are correct, and that each recipient is still a resident to whom a billing should be sent.

A much more interesting issue is the *allowance for doubtful accounts*, which is a *contra account* that is paired with and offsets the accounts receivable account. This is based on estimates of how well the CIRA can pursue assessment payments from both the current unit owner or the subsequent buyer of a unit. When an assessment is considered uncollectible, it is written off against the allowance. For example, a historical review of collections shows that a homeowners' association should maintain an allowance for doubtful accounts of 4% of its monthly assessment billings. At the end of the current month, the allowance is low by $20,000, so the accountant records the following entry:

	Debit	Credit
Bad debt expense (expense)	20,000	
Allowance for doubtful accounts (contra account)		20,000

A few weeks later, it becomes apparent that a specific assessment billing for $500 is definitely not collectible, so the accountant writes it off against the allowance with the following entry:

	Debit	Credit
Allowance for doubtful accounts (contra account)	500	
Accounts receivable (asset)		500

The Replacement Fund

Before proceeding any further, it may be useful to discuss the replacement fund, which is the reason for a large part of the assessments billed to residents.

A CIRA will need to periodically assess the condition of all common area property via a reserve study. This study involves inventorying the common property, assessing its current condition, estimating its remaining life, and then estimating its replacement cost. This information is used to derive a recommended replacement fund, from which payments are made to conduct periodic replacements. The periodic reserve study is used to derive the amount of any assessments charged to members.

The ending balance in a replacement fund is presented in a CIRA's balance sheet as an appropriation of retained earnings. Here is a sample of what the presentation might look like:

Members' equity	
Designated for future repairs and maintenance	$100,000
Undesignated	15,000
	$85,000

Accounting for Prepaid Expenses

The main expense that a CIRA is likely to pay in advance is insurance premiums. This may be a significant amount, and may be paid for in advance for an entire year. If so, the accountant should initially record the entire amount as a short-term asset, and then charge it to expense on a pro rata basis over the period covered by the insurance. The same treatment should be applied to any expenditure made in advance (such as for lawn mowing or snow removal services), though it may be easier to charge immaterial amounts to expense as incurred. For example, a CIRA pays $60,000 in property insurance at the beginning of the year, which is recorded with the following entry:

	Debit	Credit
Prepaid expenses (asset)	60,000	
Cash (asset)		60,000

In each subsequent month, $1/12^{th}$ of this amount is charged to insurance expense, using the following entry:

	Debit	Credit
Insurance expense (expense)	5,000	
Prepaid expenses (asset)		5,000

Accounting for CIRA Deposits

A CIRA was probably required to pay a deposit for various utilities. These amounts should be recorded in a long-term Deposits asset account, just to keep track of them. These amounts are so small that they could even be charged to expense as incurred, except that this eliminates any record of their existence. If one of the underlying services is to be cancelled within the next year, then the related deposit should be classified as a short-term asset. For example, a CIRA pays a $1,000 deposit to the local power company, and records it with this entry:

	Debit	Credit
Deposits (asset)	1,000	
Cash (asset)		1,000

Accounting for Inventories

A CIRA may maintain modest quantities of inventory on hand, such as when it stocks member amenities for its health club or golf course. If so, these items are to be recorded at the lower of their cost or net realizable value (known as LCM). Net realizable value is the expected selling price of something in the ordinary course of business, less the costs of completion, selling, and transportation. Given the amount of inventory that a CIRA is likely to have, its inventory balance will probably be quite small.

EXAMPLE

Mulligan Estates resells five major brands of golf clubs to its golf club members, which are noted in the following table. At the end of the year, Mulligan's accountant calculates the upper and lower price boundaries of the LCM rule for each of the products, as noted in the table:

Product	Selling Price	-	Completion/ Selling Cost	=	Upper Price Boundary	-	Normal Profit	=	Lower Price Boundary
Free Swing	$250		$25		$225		$75		$150
Golf Elite	190		19		171		57		114
Hi-Flight	150		15		135		45		90
Iridescent	1,000		100		900		300		600
Titanium	700		70		630		210		420

The normal profit associated with these products is a 30% margin on the original selling price.

The information in the preceding table for the upper and lower price boundaries is then included in the following table, which completes the LCM calculation:

Product	Upper Price Boundary	Lower Price Boundary	Existing Recognized Cost	Replacement Cost*	Market Value**	Lower of Cost or Market
Free Swing	$225	$150	$140	$260	$225	$140
Golf Elite	171	114	180	175	171	171
Hi-Flight	135	90	125	110	110	110
Iridescent	900	600	850	550	600	600
Titanium	630	420	450	390	420	420

* The cost at which the item could be acquired on the open market
** The replacement cost, as limited by the upper and lower pricing boundaries

The LCM decisions noted in the last table are explained as follows:

- *Free Swing clubs*. It would cost Mulligan $260 to replace these clubs, which is above the upper price boundary of $225. This means the market value for the purposes of this calculation is $225. Since the market price is higher than the existing recognized cost, the LCM decision is to leave the recognized cost at $140 each.
- *Golf Elite clubs*. The replacement cost of these clubs has declined to a level below the existing recognized cost, so the LCM decision is to revise the recognized cost to $171. This amount is a small reduction from the unadjusted replacement cost of $175 to the upper price boundary of $171.
- *Hi-Flight clubs*. The replacement cost is less than the recognized cost, and is between the price boundaries. Consequently, there is no need to revise the replacement cost. The LCM decision is to revise the recognized cost to $110.
- *Iridescent clubs*. The replacement cost of these clubs is below the existing recognized cost, but is below the lower price boundary. Thus, the LCM decision is to set the market price at the lower price boundary, which will be the revised cost of the clubs.
- *Titanium clubs*. The replacement cost is much less than the existing recognized cost, but also well below the lower price boundary. The LCM decision is therefore to set the market price at the lower price boundary, which is also the new product cost.

Accounting for Unit Week Inventory

A timeshare association may have a number of unit weeks deeded back to it. If so, the association should record them in a Unit Week Inventory account until they have been sold. These unit weeks should be recorded at their fair value as of the acquisition date, minus any estimated selling costs. The association can then recognize a gain or loss on the difference between this adjusted fair value amount and the aggregate amount of any associated costs of acquiring the unit weeks and any unpaid assessments on them. The accountant can obtain the fair value information for this entry from recent sales records for other timeshare units.

Accounting for Fixed Assets

There are multiple unique fixed asset issues that a CIRA must deal with, including exactly which assets it can capitalize, how it should value them, and whether there are any asset retirement obligations to account for. These and other issues are covered in the following sub-sections.

Asset Capitalization

A CIRA generally does not have many fixed assets, since the bulk of the property it oversees is owned by its residents. This is not the case for certain common property, however. A CIRA can capitalize common real property if it has title to the property in question, and either:

- It has the ability to dispose of these assets and retain the proceeds, or;
- The property is used by residents or non-residents to generate significant cash flows.

The following example illustrates this asset recognition issue.

EXAMPLE

Sunshine Estates is a planned development with an equestrian center that is valued at $12 million. The CIRA has title to the equestrian center and charges fees to both its residents and non-members. These fees sum to about $800,000 per year. Since the CIRA has title to the property and generates significant income from it, Sunshine Estates can capitalize the equestrian center.

Dingle Dell Estates is also a planned development with an equestrian center that is valued at $6 million. The CIRA also has title to the equestrian center, but only charges modest fees to non-members. Residents have access to the facilities for free. The cost of maintenance is taken on by the CIRA's standard annual assessment. In this case, the equestrian center cannot be capitalized by Dingle Dell, because the center does not generate significant revenues.

Note: Once a CIRA has capitalized an asset, it should continue to recognize it as such, including the associated depreciation, even if there is a change in the use of the asset. Thus, an asset that was originally capitalized because it generated significant cash flows should remain capitalized in later years, even if it no longer generates cash flows.

Condominiums rarely capitalize any common property, since the unit owners typically hold title to the property.

The situation is much clearer when it comes to personal property. Any type of CIRA can capitalize and depreciate personal property, such as maintenance equipment, recreational equipment, and work vehicles. A time-share association may own the interior furnishings in its units, in which case it can capitalize and depreciate them.

Generally, a cooperative will capitalize and depreciate nearly all assets, since it directly owns the property.

> **Tip:** Given the variety of issues relating to the capitalization of assets, a CIRA should adopt a standard capitalization policy, in which it states the capitalization limit above which expenditures can be capitalized, the useful life to be used for each asset class, and which types of assets can be capitalized.

Interest Capitalization

If a CIRA constructs assets for its own use, it should capitalize all related interest costs into the cost of the asset. Doing so provides a truer picture of the total investment in an asset. Follow these steps to calculate the amount of interest to be capitalized for a specific project:

1. Construct a table itemizing the amounts of expenditures made and the dates on which the expenditures were made.
2. Determine the date on which interest capitalization ends.
3. Calculate the capitalization period for each expenditure, which is the number of days between the specific expenditure and the end of the interest capitalization period.
4. Divide each capitalization period by the total number of days elapsed between the date of the first expenditure and the end of the interest capitalization period to arrive at the capitalization multiplier for each line item.
5. Multiply each expenditure amount by its capitalization multiplier to arrive at the average expenditure for each line item over the capitalization measurement period.
6. Add up the average expenditures at the line-item level to arrive at a grand total average expenditure.
7. If there is project-specific debt, multiply the grand total of the average expenditures by the interest rate on that debt to arrive at the capitalized interest related to that debt.
8. If the grand total of the average expenditures exceeds the amount of the project-specific debt, multiply the excess expenditure amount by the weighted average of the CIRA's other outstanding debt to arrive at the remaining amount of interest to be capitalized.
9. Add together both capitalized interest calculations. If the combined total is more than the total interest cost incurred by the CIRA during the calculation period, reduce the amount of interest to be capitalized to the total interest cost incurred during the calculation period.
10. Record the interest capitalization with a debit to the project's fixed asset account and a credit to the interest expense account.

EXAMPLE

Somnolent Estates is building a golf course and clubhouse. Somnolent makes payments related to the project of $10,000,000 and $14,000,000 to a contractor on January 1 and July 1, respectively. The facilities are completed on December 31.

For the 12-month period of construction, Somnolent can capitalize all of the interest on the $10,000,000 payment, since it was outstanding during the full period of construction. Somnolent can capitalize the interest on the $14,000,000 payment for half of the construction period, since it was outstanding during only the second half of the period. The average expenditure for which the interest cost can be capitalized is calculated in the following table:

Date of Payment	Expenditure Amount	Capitalization Period*	Capitalization Multiplier	Average Expenditure
January 1	$10,000,000	12 months	12/12 months = 100%	$10,000,000
July 1	14,000,000	6 months	6/12 months = 50%	7,000,000
				$17,000,000

* In the table, the capitalization period is defined as the number of months that elapse between the expenditure payment date and the end of the interest capitalization period.

The only debt that Somnolent has outstanding during this period is a line of credit, on which the interest rate is 8%. The maximum amount of interest that it can capitalize into the cost of this project is $1,360,000, which is calculated as:

8% Interest rate × $17,000,000 Average expenditure = $1,360,000

Somnolent records the following journal entry:

	Debit	Credit
Fixed assets – Golf course and clubhouse (asset)	1,360,000	
Interest expense (expense)		1,360,000

Tip: There may be an inordinate number of expenditures related to a larger project, which could result in a large and unwieldy calculation of average expenditures. To reduce the workload, consider aggregating these expenses by month, and then assume that each expenditure was made in the middle of the month, thereby reducing all of the expenditures for each month to a single line item.

Note: Interest capitalization should only be used when construction covers a long period of time. Doing so for projects that span only a short period of time would result in a large amount of accounting effort to capitalize a relatively small interest cost.

Asset Valuation

When a CIRA acquires common property, it should value the property at its acquisition cost. This cost includes anything that makes the asset ready for use, including sales taxes, transport charges, transport insurance, and installation costs.

If it is not possible to obtain information about the acquisition cost, then it is permissible to instead use an insurance appraisal, cost appraisal, property tax appraisal, or some similar method. This should be a one-time event, which is only used to establish the initial cost of the asset.

In cases where the developer transfers assets to a CIRA, they should be recorded at their fair value as of the acquisition date. If information about the developer's cost is available, this can be taken into consideration when developing the fair value. *Fair value* is the price that two parties are willing to pay for an asset or liability, preferably in an active market.

The ideal conditions are not always available for obtaining the fair value of an asset. Consequently, *GAAP* provides a hierarchy of information sources that range from Level 1 (best) to Level 3 (worst). The general intent of these levels of information is to step the accountant through a series of valuation alternatives, where solutions closer to Level 1 are preferred over Level 3. The characteristics of the three levels are as follows:

- *Level 1*. This is a quoted price for an identical item in an active market on the measurement date. This is the most reliable evidence of fair value, and should be used whenever this information is available. It may be necessary to adjust a Level 1 input when a quoted price does not represent fair value, as may be the case when significant events alter the price that parties are willing to pay. When a quoted Level 1 price is adjusted, doing so automatically shifts the result into a lower level.
- *Level 2*. This is directly or indirectly observable inputs other than quoted prices. This definition includes prices for assets or liabilities that are (with key items noted in bold):
  - For **similar** items in active markets; or
  - For identical or similar items in **inactive** markets; or
  - For inputs **other than** quoted prices, such as credit spreads and interest rates; or
  - For inputs **derived from** correlation with observable market data.

An example of a Level 2 input is a valuation multiple for a business unit that is based on the sale of comparable entities. Another example is the price per square foot for a building, based on prices involving comparable facilities in similar locations.

It may be necessary to adjust the information derived from Level 2 inputs, since it does not exactly match the assets for which fair values are being derived. Adjustments may be needed for such factors as the condition or location of assets and the transaction volume of the markets from which information is derived.

- *Level 3*. This is an unobservable input. It may include the CIRA's own data, adjusted for other reasonably available information. These inputs should reflect the assumptions that would be used by market participants to formulate prices, including assumptions about risk. Examples of a Level 3 input are an internally-generated financial forecast and the prices contained within an offered quote from a distributor.

The information sources in Level 1 are considered to supply the most objective information to the derivation of fair value information, since they are coming from the marketplace. Conversely, the information sources in Level 3 are considered to supply the most subjective information, since they are largely derived internally.

These three levels are known as the fair value hierarchy. Please note that these three levels are only used to select inputs to valuation techniques (which are covered next). The different types of fair value measurement approaches are outlined below:

- *Market approach*. Uses the prices associated with actual market transactions for similar or identical assets and liabilities to derive a fair value. For example, the prices of securities held can be obtained from a national exchange on which these securities are routinely bought and sold. Another possibility is to derive a valuation based on market multiples that come from a set of comparable transactions.
- *Income approach*. Uses estimated future cash flows or earnings, adjusted by a discount rate that represents the time value of money and the risk of cash flows not being achieved, to derive a discounted present value. These cash flows would come from renting a unit and/or by selling it at some point in the future. An alternative way to incorporate risk into this approach is to develop a probability-weighted-average set of possible future cash flows. Option pricing models can also be used under the income approach.
- *Cost approach*. Uses the estimated cost to replace an asset (or the capabilities of the asset), adjusted for the obsolescence of the existing asset. The obsolescence concept includes the deterioration of an asset, its technological obsolescence, and its economic obsolescence.

Valuation of Abandoned Units

A condominium or a homeowners' association might receive an abandoned unit as a result of a lien[1] related to an unpaid assessment. In this situation, the CIRA records the unit at its fair value as of the foreclosure date, minus the estimated cost to resell it. If there is a difference between this fair value and the amount of the unpaid assessment and any assumed debt, the CIRA recognizes a gain or loss on the difference. These assets would be recorded in an "Investment in Real Estate" asset account.

---

[1] A CIRA will apply a lien against a unit in order to recover the amount of any unpaid assessments, interest costs, penalties, and attorneys' fees when the unit is eventually sold. Depending on state law, it may be possible for a CIRA to foreclose an assessment lien, triggering the immediate sale of the associated unit.

Valuation of Purchased Units

A CIRA might elect to bid on a unit that is in foreclosure. If it wins the bid and takes possession of the unit, it should develop a fair value for the unit that should take into account its expected future cash flows. The CIRA then records this fair value figure as an asset. If the CIRA expects to sell the unit, then the unit's fair value should be reduced by the expected selling costs[2]. Furthermore, the cost of any repairs that will increase the value of the unit should also be capitalized.

If there is a difference between this value and the consideration paid to acquire the unit, the CIRA should record the difference as a credit to a gain account, such as Gain on Acquired Foreclosed Unit. The CIRA should then begin depreciating the unit, and should conduct periodic impairment testing to see if its fair value subsequently drops below its carrying amount.

Asset Depreciation

When fixed assets can be capitalized by a CIRA, they should be depreciated based on their estimated useful lives. This is typically done using straight-line depreciation for most assets. Under the straight-line method of depreciation, recognize depreciation expense evenly over the estimated useful life of the asset. The straight-line calculation steps are:

1. Subtract the estimated salvage value of the asset from the amount at which it is recorded on the books.
2. Determine the estimated useful life of the asset. It is easiest to use a standard useful life for each class of assets.
3. Divide the estimated useful life (in years) into 1 to arrive at the straight-line depreciation rate.
4. Multiply the depreciation rate by the asset cost (less salvage value).

EXAMPLE

Penzance Estates purchases a street cleaner for $60,000. It has an estimated salvage value of $10,000 and a useful life of five years. The accountant calculates the annual straight-line depreciation for the machine as:

1. Purchase cost of $60,000 – Estimated salvage value of $10,000 = Depreciable asset cost of $50,000
2. $1 \div 5$-Year useful life = 20% Depreciation rate per year
3. 20% Depreciation rate × $50,000 Depreciable asset cost = $10,000 Annual depreciation

---

[2] Selling costs include legal fees, transfer fees, closing costs, and the selling commission.

The annual depreciation entry is:

	Debit	Credit
Depreciation expense (expense)	10,000	
Accumulated depreciation (contra asset)		10,000

Asset Impairment

A CIRA is supposed to periodically review its fixed assets to see if their valuations are impaired. This situation arises when the carrying amount of an asset is greater than its fair value. When this situation arises, the accountant should write down the carrying amount of the asset to its fair value. For example, a homeowners' association should periodically conduct an impairment analysis on its clubhouse, while a coop would need to do so for its entire apartment building.

At a minimum, impairment testing should be conducted once a year. In addition, this testing could be conducted whenever conditions or events indicate that the carrying amount of an asset might no longer be recoverable. The carrying amount is not considered to be recoverable when it is greater than the sum of the expected undiscounted cash flows that can be expected from the continued use and/or disposition of the asset.

Asset Retirement Obligations

A CIRA may need to recognize an obligation to retire an asset as of some future date. This is only done when it is possible to derive a reasonable estimate of the fair value of this obligation. For example, if there is an environmental regulation requiring a CIRA to eventually remove the fuel tank used to power a backup generator, then it must recognize a liability for this retirement. This liability is recognized as soon as the CIRA incurs the obligation, such as when the governing environmental regulation is passed by the state legislature. The accounting for asset retirement obligations is extensive; see the author's *Fixed Asset Accounting* course for more information.

Insurance Settlements

A CIRA might occasionally receive an insurance settlement when insured assets have been destroyed. If so, it can only record an insurance recovery when the recovery claim is probable and the amount can be reasonably estimated. The receipt of a claim is not considered to be probable when a claim is still to be litigated or discussions about a settlement payment are ongoing. If the payment can be recognized, and the CIRA has not capitalized the related assets, then the settlement proceeds would be recognized as revenue. However, if the CIRA has capitalized the related assets, then the CIRA must recognize a gain or loss on the transaction. In the latter scenario, the gain or loss is calculated as the difference between the carrying amount of the capitalized asset and the settlement received from the insurer.

> **Tip:** A CIRA may need to spend money immediately to fix damage caused by a natural disaster, while the associated insurance payout may not arrive for months – or longer. To properly track these expenditures against their offsetting insurance payouts, we suggest recording these items in a separate fund.

If a CIRA receives an insurance payout on behalf of its residents for their property, it can act as a pass-through and pay each of them their share of the proceeds. Or, it can retain the funds and use them to directly pay for repairs to the residents' property.

Leased Assets

A CIRA may enter into a variety of leasing arrangements, such as for equipment rentals, storage space, and office space. A central concept of the accounting for leases is that the CIRA (the lessee) should recognize the assets and liabilities that underlie each leasing arrangement. This concept results in the following recognition in the balance sheet of the lessee as of the lease commencement date:

- Recognize a liability to make lease payments to the lessor
- Recognize a right-of-use asset that represents the right of the lessee to use the leased asset during the lease term

There are a number of additional topics related to asset and liability recognition, which are covered in the following sub-sections.

Types of Leases

There are several types of lease designations, which differ if an entity is the lessee or the lessor. It is critical to determine the type of a lease, since the accounting varies by lease type. The choices for a **lessee** are that a lease can be designated as either a finance lease or an operating lease. In essence, a *finance lease* designation implies that the lessee has purchased the underlying asset (even though this may not actually be the case), while an *operating lease* designation implies that the lessee has obtained the use of the underlying asset for only a period of time. A lessee should classify a lease as a finance lease when any of the following criteria are met:

- *Ownership transfer*. Ownership of the underlying asset is shifted to the lessee by the end of the lease term.
- *Ownership option*. The lessee has a purchase option to buy the leased asset, and is reasonably certain to use it.
- *Lease term*. The lease term covers the major part of the underlying asset's remaining economic life. This is considered to be 75% or more of the remaining economic life of the underlying asset. This criterion is not valid if the lease commencement date is near the end of the asset's economic life, which is considered to be a date that falls within the last 25% of the underlying asset's total economic life.

- *Present value*. The present value of the sum of all lease payments and any lessee-guaranteed residual value matches or exceeds the fair value of the underlying asset. The present value is based on the interest rate implicit in the lease.
- *Specialization*. The asset is so specialized that it has no alternative use for the lessor following the lease term. In this situation, there are essentially no remaining benefits that revert to the lessor.

When none of the preceding criteria are met, the lessee must classify a lease as an operating lease.

Initial Measurement

As of the commencement date of a lease, the lessee measures the liability and the right-of-use asset associated with the lease. These measurements are derived as follows:

- *Lease liability*. The present value of the lease payments, discounted at the discount rate for the lease. This rate is the rate implicit in the lease when that rate is readily determinable. If not, the lessee instead uses its incremental borrowing rate.
- *Right-of-use asset*. The initial amount of the lease liability, plus any lease payments made to the lessor before the lease commencement date, plus any initial direct costs incurred, minus any lease incentives received.

EXAMPLE

Insufficient Estates enters into a five-year lease, where the lease payments are $35,000 per year, payable at the end of each year. Insufficient incurs initial direct costs of $8,000. The rate implicit in the lease is 8%.

At the commencement of the lease, the lease liability is $139,745, which is calculated as $35,000 multiplied by the 3.9927 rate for the five-period present value of an ordinary annuity. The right-of-use asset is calculated as the lease liability plus the amount of the initial direct costs, for a total of $147,745.

Short-Term Leases

When a lease has a term of 12 months or less, the lessee can elect not to recognize lease-related assets and liabilities in the balance sheet. This election is made by class of asset. When a lessee makes this election, it should usually recognize the expense related to a lease on a straight-line basis over the term of the lease.

If the lease term changes so that the remaining term now extends more than 12 months beyond the end of the previously determined lease term or the lessee will likely purchase the underlying asset, the arrangement is no longer considered a short-term lease. In this situation, account for the lease as a longer-term lease as of the date when there was a change in circumstances.

Finance Leases

When a lessee has designated a lease as a finance lease, it should recognize the following over the term of the lease:

- The ongoing amortization of the right-of-use asset
- The ongoing amortization of the interest on the lease liability
- Any variable lease payments that are not included in the lease liability
- Any impairment of the right-of-use asset

The amortization period for the right-of-use asset is from the lease commencement date to the earlier of the end of the lease term or the end of the useful life of the asset. An exception is when it is reasonably certain that the lessee will exercise an option to purchase the asset, in which case the amortization period is through the end of the asset's useful life.

After the commencement date, the lessee increases the carrying amount of the lease liability to include the interest expense on the lease liability, while reducing the carrying amount by the amount of all lease payments made during the period. The interest on the lease liability is the amount that generates a constant periodic discount rate on the remaining liability balance.

After the commencement date, the lessee reduces the right-of-use asset by the amount of accumulated amortization and accumulated impairment (if any).

EXAMPLE

Scottish Estates agrees to a five-year lease of equipment that requires an annual $20,000 payment, due at the end of each year. At the end of the lease period, Scottish has the option to buy the equipment for $1,000. Since the expected residual value of the equipment at that time is expected to be $25,000, the large discount makes it reasonably certain that the purchase option will be exercised. At the commencement date of the lease, the fair value of the equipment is $120,000, with an economic life of eight years. The discount rate for the lease is 6%.

Scottish classifies the lease as a finance lease, since it is reasonably certain to exercise the purchase option.

The lease liability at the commencement date is $84,995, which is calculated as the present value of five payments of $20,000, plus the present value of the $1,000 purchase option payment, discounted at 6%. Scottish recognizes the right-of-use asset as the same amount, since there are no initial direct costs, lease incentives, or other types of payments made by Scottish, either at or before the commencement date.

Scottish amortizes the right-of-use asset over the eight-year expected useful life of the equipment, under the assumption that it will exercise the purchase option and therefore keep the equipment for the eight-year period.

As an example of the subsequent accounting for the lease, Scottish recognizes a first-year interest expense of $5,100 (calculated as 6% × $84,995 lease liability), and recognizes the amortization of the right-of-use asset in the amount of $10,624 (calculated as $84,995 ÷ 8 years). This results in a lease liability at the end of Year 1 that has been reduced to $70,095 (calculated as $84,995 + $5,100 interest - $20,000 lease payment) and a right-of-use asset that has been reduced to $74,371 (calculated as $84,995 - $10,624 amortization).

By the end of Year 5, which is when the lease terminates, the lease liability has been reduced to $1,000, which is the amount of the purchase option. Scottish exercises the option, which settles the remaining liability. At that time, the carrying amount of the right-of-use asset has declined to $31,875 (reflecting five years of amortization at $10,624 per year). Scottish shifts this amount into a fixed asset account, and depreciates it over the remaining three years of its useful life.

Operating Leases

When a lessee has designated a lease as an operating lease, the lessee should recognize the following over the term of the lease:

- A lease cost in each period, where the total cost of the lease is allocated over the lease term on a straight-line basis. This can be altered if there is another systematic and rational basis of allocation that more closely follows the benefit usage pattern to be derived from the underlying asset.
- Any variable lease payments that are not included in the lease liability
- Any impairment of the right-of-use asset

EXAMPLE

Nevermore Estates enters into an operating lease in which the lease payment is $25,000 per year for the first five years and $30,000 per year for the next five years. These payments sum to $275,000 over ten years. Nevermore will therefore recognize a lease expense of $27,500 per year for all of the years in the lease term.

At any point in the life of an operating lease, the remaining cost of the lease is considered to be the total lease payments, plus all initial direct costs associated with the lease, minus the lease cost already recognized in previous periods.

After the commencement date, the lessee measures the lease liability at the present value of the lease payments that have not yet been made, using the same discount rate that was established at the commencement date.

After the commencement date, the lessee measures the right-of-use asset at the amount of the lease liability, adjusted for the following items:

- Any impairment of the asset
- Prepaid or accrued lease payments
- Any remaining balance of lease incentives received
- Any unamortized initial direct costs

EXAMPLE

Hinklesville Estates enters into a 10-year operating lease for offices and storage space. The annual lease payment is $40,000 to be paid at the end of each year. The CIRA incurs initial direct costs of $8,000, and receives $15,000 from the lessor as a lease incentive. Hinklesville's incremental borrowing rate is 6%. The initial direct costs and lease incentive will be amortized over the 10 years of the lease term.

Hinklesville measures the lease liability as the present value of the 10 lease payments at a 6% discount rate, which is $294,404. The right-of-use asset is measured at $287,404, which is the initial $294,404 measurement, plus the initial direct costs of $8,000, minus the lease incentive of $15,000.

After one year, the carrying amount of the lease liability is $272,068, which is the present value of the remaining nine lease payments at a 6% discount rate. The carrying amount of the right-of-use asset is $265,768, which is the amount of the liability, plus the unamortized initial direct costs of $7,200, minus the remaining balance of the lease incentive of $13,500.

Optional Lease Payments

When there is an optional payment in a lease agreement that can be made by the lessee to purchase a leased asset, this optional payment is only included in the recognition of assets and liabilities if it is reasonably certain that the lessee will exercise the purchase option.

Right-of-Use Asset Impairment

If a right-of-use asset is determined to be impaired, the impairment is immediately recorded, thereby reducing the carrying amount of the asset. Its subsequent measurement is calculated as the carrying amount immediately after the impairment transaction, minus any subsequent accumulated amortization.

EXAMPLE

Frogmorton Estates enters into a five-year equipment lease that is classified as an operating lease. At the end of Year 2, when the carrying amount of the lease liability and the right-of-use asset are both $100,000, the accountant determines that the asset is impaired, and recognizes an impairment loss of $70,000. This reduces the carrying amount of the asset to $30,000.

Beginning in Year 3 and continuing through the remainder of the lease term, Frogmorton amortizes the right-of-use asset at a rate of $10,000 per year, which will bring the carrying amount of the asset to zero by the end of the lease term.

Derecognition

At the termination of a lease, the right-of-use asset and associated lease liability are removed from the books. The difference between the two amounts is accounted for as a profit or loss at that time. If the lessee purchases the underlying asset at the termination of a lease, then any difference between the purchase price and the lease liability is recorded as an adjustment to the asset's carrying amount.

If a lessee subleases an underlying asset and the terms of the original agreement then relieve the lessee of the primary lease obligation, this is considered a termination of the original lease.

Liability Accounting

The bulk of the liability-related accounting for a CIRA is typical accounts payable transactions for which the usual entry is a credit to the accounts payable liability account and a debit to the applicable expense or asset account. However, there are still some interesting liability issues pertaining to CIRAs, which we address in the following sub-sections.

Refundable Security Deposits

A CIRA may keep a record of the refundable security deposits received from its residents. These deposits may include quite large deposits related to architectural issues, which are only returned after a compliance concern has been remediated. Lesser deposits may be collected for clubhouse rentals, keys, and similar items. The basic accounting is quite simple – accept a deposit in relation to a specific issue, and pay it back when the issue is resolved. However, when deposits are poorly documented, it is easy to lose track of the money. For example, a resident might move away without reclaiming a deposit, which then sits on the CIRA's books forever. At this point, a deposit should be classified as unclaimed property, and forwarded to the state government's unclaimed property fund. These excess deposit amounts should not be cleared off the books with an offsetting entry to revenue, since this could be illegal under the state's escheat laws.

Assessments Received in Advance

Many timeshares issue annual billings for maintenance fees well before the fiscal year to which they apply. If so, the related receivable should be reversed and removed from the entity's balance sheet until the start of the applicable fiscal year, since the receivable is not a valid asset until that time. In addition, if any residents pay these billed amounts prior to the start of the applicable period, then these amounts should be recorded as a deferred revenue liability of the timeshare association.

Property Tax Liabilities

The billing of property taxes by the applicable government entity will depend on the practices of this entity. It may be billed in total to the CIRA, which then incorporates this charge into its annual assessments to residents. Or, the government may bill residents directly. In the latter case, there is no accounting entry for the CIRA. In the former case, the CIRA records a liability for the property taxes in a separate real estate taxes fund, which is reduced by resident payments. Or, property tax transactions are simply included in the operating fund – though this may clutter up the fund with an excessive number of entries.

If the CIRA has been directly billed for the full amount of property tax, it is likely that the amount of offsetting payments from residents will result in a shortfall in the amount to be remitted to the government; this is because some residents do not pay. When this is the case, the CIRA usually pays the difference from the operating fund, which is then treated as a receivable of the operating fund.

Debt Accounting

A CIRA may obtain a loan in order to pay for construction defects, a common property replacement, or perhaps a common property upgrade. The repayment terms on these loans can be rather flexible, depending on the timing of the assessments used to pay for them. This can allow a CIRA to make an annual payment against a loan based on the funds received from an assessment, after which the loan is reamortized, which alters the remaining debt balance.

If borrowed funds are to be used for repairs and asset replacements, then the debt should be recorded within the replacement fund. Alternatively, if the borrowed funds are intended for asset acquisitions that are to be capitalized in the operating fund, then the debt should be recorded in that fund.

> **Note:** A cooperative typically has a mortgage outstanding on its real property.

Equity Accounting

Several equity transactions that the accountant for a CIRA might encounter are noted below.

Common Stock

A coop is created as a corporation, and so it issues shares to its residents. This is not the case for condominium organizations, homeowners' associations, and some types of timeshare associations, since they do not issue shares.

There may be cases in which coop tenants are forced by their financial circumstances to surrender their shares in the coop corporation. If so, and the tenants have not paid their assessments, then the returned shares are recorded by the coop as treasury stock at its cost – which includes forgiveness of the assessment receivable and the coop's related legal costs. However, if a tenant gives back the shares as a gift (usually at the end of their lease term), then the treasury stock is recorded at its fair value as of the transfer date. Alternatively, if the coop elects to buy back shares in order to resell them at a later date, then the shares should be recorded at their purchase price.

Contributed Capital

A CIRA may receive contributions of capital, usually in the form of common area property that is donated by the developer. Depending on the organization, capital may also come from new residents, which they are required to contribute when they purchase a unit. It is also possible that residents will purchase property and then donate it to the CIRA, which is accounted for as contributed capital. In all cases, these contributions are treated as a debit to either the cash account or a property account, and a credit to the contributed capital account.

Distributions of Capital

A distribution of capital may arise when a CIRA refunds the excess amount of a special or normal assessment back to residents.

Accounting for Revenue

A CIRA cannot recognize revenue unless it has a contract with the parties being billed. The underlying basis for revenue recognition for a CIRA is its governing documents, which entitle it to assess residents for the cost of the services it provides; this constitutes a contract, so the CIRA can bill residents for amounts authorized within the governing documents, and recognize revenue from those billings.

A further consideration for a CIRA is customer credit risk. Revenue cannot be recognized unless it is probable that it will collect substantially all of the consideration stated in its billings to residents. This can be a problem, since a CIRA rarely gets to choose its residents – instead, it is stuck with whomever purchased property. In this case, the CIRA could evaluate the creditworthiness of its residents, perhaps based on its historical collections experience, to decide whether it will probably collect from them. When some assessments are not expected to be collected, revenue should not be recognized for this amount. Even after this conservative accounting, there may still be a need for an allowance for uncollectible assessments. If so, the balance sheet presentation of this allowance could be displayed using the following format:

Assessments receivable, less allowance for doubtful accounts of $8,000 $235,000

> **Note:** A timeshare association might have a substantial allowance for uncollectible assessments, since many timeshare owners are trying to get out of their annual maintenance responsibilities.

Some receivables may not be difficult to collect over the long term, if state law allows a CIRA to collect overdue receivables from residents or buyers as part of the foreclosure and resale process for a unit.

Yet another issue is how to allocate an assessment to the various services being billed. This billed amount should be derived from the services costs contained within a CIRA's annual budget, so it should be relatively easy to apportion the revenue from an assessment back to the various services accounts, based on the proportions stated in the budget. Also, this performance obligation by the CIRA is generally considered to be spread evenly throughout the year, so there is no need to defer the recognition of any billed assessments. In short, operating assessments should be recognized as revenue in the period to which the assessment applies.

If assessments are billed on a monthly basis (typically on the first business day of the month), then it is likely that the full amount billed can be recognized for that month. However, if the assessment is for a longer period, such as a quarter, then the revenue needs to be recognized equitably over the full term covered by the assessment. Thus, for a quarterly assessment billing, the CIRA will be able to recognize one-third of the billed amount in each of the three months comprising the quarter.

There may also be cases in which assessment payments are received in advance of the period to which they apply. For example, an annual assessment might be billed a month before the new year, with some residents paying prior to the new year. In this case, the received funds are initially classified as a liability, and then converted to revenue over the course of the assessment period. In the meantime, these funds are stored in a short-term liability account with an explanatory title, such as Prepaid Assessments, or perhaps Deferred Revenue. For example, a CIRA bills its residents $90,000 in assessments for the first quarter of the year, of which $10,000 is received before the start of the year. The entry to record this as a liability is as follows:

	Debit	Credit
Cash (asset)	10,000	
Prepaid assessments (liability)		10,000

There is not yet an entry to accounts receivable, since the billing was dated for January 1, which was later that the receipt date of the funds. The remainder of the money is paid in January, resulting in several entries. First, the initial entry to a liability account is reversed in January with the following entry:

	Debit	Credit
Prepaid assessments (liability)	10,000	
Cash (asset)		10,000

Next, the accountant records the issuance of billings to residents, and the initial recognition of revenue, with the following entry:

	Debit	Credit
Accounts receivable (asset)	90,000	
Revenue (revenue)		90,000

Then, when residents pay their bills, the accountant records the full receipt of cash for the invoiced amounts, with the following entry:

	Debit	Credit
Cash (asset)	90,000	
Accounts receivable (asset)		90,000

Next, the accountant records two-thirds of the initially-recorded revenue as being a deferred revenue liability, since it relates to February and March. The entry is:

	Debit	Credit
Revenue (revenue)	60,000	
Deferred revenue (liability)		60,000

Note: In cases where assessment billings cover both charges for ongoing operations and future repairs and replacements, be sure to allocate the assessment payments between operations and the replacement fund.

What about the revenue recognition for assessments related to major repairs and replacements? In this case, the performance obligation is considered to be complete when the related funds have been expended – such as when a replacement roof has been installed. The full amount of revenue related to the assessment can only be recognized when this has occurred. Any unspent funds in the reserve account are classified as a liability of the CIRA, since they are deferred revenue. However, any excess assessments that will not be used after all expenditures have been made can be recognized as revenue. If the CIRA elects to instead apply the excess assessment to the following year's assessment (a common practice), then no revenue recognition entry is made.

Note: If you shift funds from the operating fund to a replacement reserve, do not classify this transfer as a deferred revenue liability, since it was already recognized as revenue in the operating fund before it was transferred.

Resident Assessments

A key accounting issue is the percentage interest assigned to each resident in cases where there is common property for which they must pay a pro rata proportion of the upkeep costs. This percentage was initially set by the developer, who assigns the percentage (either based on unit value or size). On occasion, the percentage will be weighted based on additional factors, such as a unit's location within a development.

Note: The percentage interest assigned to a resident may decline over time, as additional units are completed and added to the CIRA.

The governing documents also describe which types of expenses are considered to be common expenses. Once these expenses have been defined, they are included in the assessment cost pool, for allocation out to the residents. The exact amount of these expenses will be included in the annual budget, which is the basis for the assessments.

In cases where the property developer has not yet sold all units, the developer will be assigned an assessment based on the percentage interest assigned to any completed units still held by the developer. In some states, the developer is even responsible for the assessment on units that have not yet been completed.

When the CIRA assesses a property and the resident does not pay it, then the CIRA can obtain a lien on that person's property. Depending on the state, this lien can be assigned a high priority (though after the mortgage lien rights), thereby giving the CIRA a good chance of being paid when the property is eventually sold.

> **Note:** For a mixed development where there are free-standing homes and townhomes, assessments may be based on classes that are linked to the maintenance requirements of each type of residence.

Special Assessments

A CIRA can issue a special assessment to its residents to cover special needs. For example, a CIRA might need to repay a loan, replace a roof, pay for litigation, or fund an operating shortfall. These funds are usually stored in a separate bank account and accounted for within a separate fund.

A CIRA should only recognize revenue for a special assessment when its related performance obligations have been completed. Typically, the performance obligation is considered to be complete when the funds have been expended for their intended purpose. Until that time, the funds are classified as a liability (deferred revenue). There are some variations on this approach, as noted in the following exhibit.

Recognition of Special Assessment Revenue

Scenario	Revenue Recognition
Assessment for common area repair	Recognize when related expenses are incurred
Assessment for repayment of debt	Recognize when debt payments are made
Assessment to fund current year projects	Recognize revenue in the period billed if obligation is met in the same period
Assessment to fund operating shortfall	Recognize revenue in the period billed if obligation is met in the same period
Assessment to fund replacement fund shortfall	Recognize revenue in the period billed if obligation is met in the same period
Assessment to pay unexpected expenses	Recognize revenue in the period billed if obligation is met in the same period

If any funds from a special assessment turn out not to be needed and are then made available for general operating purposes, then they should be recognized as revenue at that time. However, if these funds are shifted to the replacement reserve fund, then they should continue to be recorded as a liability (deferred revenue) until they are used.

A CIRA may allow residents to pay for a special assessment over time, rather than in a lump sum. If so, it can charge interest on the delayed payments, in order to pass along its own financing costs to the residents. This may require the accountant to maintain an amortization schedule for each resident that elects to pay the special assessment in installments.

In cases where a special assessment turns out to be more than needed and the CIRA decides to refund the residual amount back to residents, this refund should be accounted for as a reduction of the related deferred revenue liability.

Subsidy Agreements

The developer of a CIRA may enter into a subsidy agreement with it, whereby it agrees to make one or more subsidy payments in order to support common area amenities that would otherwise lose money until more residents buy into the community. These subsidies typically end after either a fixed period of time or after a certain number of lots have been sold. The amount of the subsidy is usually the amount required for the amenities to reach a breakeven profit level.

Transfer Fees

Coop transfer fees are charged when a tenant transfers a lease to a new party; this fee is imposed to keep tenants from acquiring cooperative units for speculative purposes. It may be charged as a flat fee, or as a percentage of the sale price. It is also known as a flip tax.

A variation on the concept is a transfer fee charged by other types of CIRAs, where the intent is to cover the costs of the CIRA in processing any unit sales, such as credit checks on new residents. In this case, the intent is not to earn a profit on a transfer – merely to cover costs.

Transfer fees should be recorded in a separate account, and may either be presented separately on the CIRA's income statement or bundled in with other miscellaneous revenue items.

Penalties for Delinquent Assessments

It is quite likely that a resident will occasionally pay an assessment late – perhaps very late. If so, the CIRA can charge interest and penalties on these delinquent assessments. Interest income should be recorded in a separate revenue account, as should any penalty payments. These accounts may be combined on the CIRA's income statement, into an Interest and Late Fees line item.

Lawsuit Settlements

A CIRA may file suit on behalf of its residents against the property developer in relation to defective construction, for which damages may be received. The CIRA might also sue the developer for nonpayment of assessments for units held by the developer prior to their sale. When these lawsuits are ongoing, the accountant should not accrue a contingent gain until it has been fully realized. Thus, the CIRA should only recognize a settlement as revenue when the developer has agreed to the settlement amount and is not going to appeal the verdict.

Rental Income

A CIRA may have taken possession of various units because of delinquent assessments. If so, it can rent out these units, which may result in a modest level of ongoing revenue.

Income on Investments

Any income earned on investments should be recognized as soon as it is earned.

Utility Pass-Throughs

It is quite common for utility companies to install master meters for their services, rather than installing individual metering for each unit. Similarly, television and Internet firms prefer to enter into a single agreement with an entire CIRA, rather than billing each resident individually. In these cases, the CIRA assesses these costs as a pass-through to the residents.

In order to bill utility costs through to residents, the CIRA has several options for determining how much to bill to each resident. For some utilities, such as trash pickup, Internet, and television, it can divide the total billing by the number of units and then assess residents using this apportionment. This approach works well when the cost consumption is the same for all units. In cases where the cost incurred differs by unit, such as with electricity, the CIRA can install meters at the individual unit level to track usage, and then apportion the billing based on usage.

There are several ways to deal with the billing of residents for utility pass-throughs. One approach is to include it in the periodic assessments being charged to residents. However, there is usually a great deal of pressure from residents to keep the assessment as low as possible, so an alternative is to bill the pass-throughs separately.

> **Note:** The CIRA might consider inflating pass-through charges slightly to offset any expected unpaid bills.

There are two ways to account for these pass-through costs. One approach is to report the expense billed to the CIRA by the utility providers as a separate expense, with its pass-through billings to residents being recorded as a separate revenue item. Another option is to net the two together, so that pass-through billings are offset against the related expense. In the latter treatment, the net effect should be quite a small reported balance. The former approach typically applies when the CIRA is directly responsible for the services being provided, which is rarely the case. Accordingly, the latter approach of netting revenue and expenses is considered the more theoretically correct accounting treatment.

Cable Provider Marketing Access Fees

A cable television provider may pay a CIRA an up-front fee to gain exclusive access to its residents. This fee is paid in advance of what is typically a multi-year access period. Since the CIRA is providing a "service" to the cable provider in the form of future access to its residents, this payment must be initially recorded as a liability (deferred revenue). For example, if a cable provider were to pay a $5,000 access fee for a five-year period, then the CIRA should recognize just $1,000 of this amount per year over the course of the five-year contract period.

Other Income

There are several other forms of income that a CIRA may recognize. Each one should be recorded in a different revenue account. For example, a CIRA might require residents to purchase an annual pass to use gym, tennis, pool, or equestrian facilities. Or, it may receive program income from conducting special events on its premises. It may also provide special services to its residents, such as cleaning services or valet parking. It may also receive income from any vending machines kept on the premises. In some cases, a CIRA might even receive lease income from cell tower or billboard operators who place these items on CIRA property.

When a CIRA is structured to also provide country club services, such as golf course operations and a restaurant, it is fairly common for the accountant to employ a second accounting system that specializes in country club accounting, rather than the software that it uses for its association activities. This can present problems, since the summary-level accounting information from the country club system must be transferred over to the association accounting system in order to compile aggregated financial reports for the CIRA.

CIRA Expenses

Most expenses incurred by a CIRA are ones that any business must deal with, such as bank fees, travel and entertainment, and office supplies. We will not address these more generic expenses, focusing instead on those that are unusually large or unique to CIRAs.

Expenses Charged Against Assessments

When assessments are levied against residents, they are typically for major repairs and replacements. Offsetting these assessments are the expenses incurred to complete the targeted repairs and replacements. Examples of these expenses are direct costs (such as construction materials), indirect costs (such as insurance costs), and allocated costs. In essence, expenses should be recognized in the fund for which they were originally budgeted. When expenses are incurred for which there was no budget, they should be recorded in whichever fund most closely relates to the nature of the expense.

Property Insurance

A substantial expense is the property insurance that covers common property, plus comprehensive liability, directors' and officers' liability, workers' compensation, and fidelity bonds.

Cost Allocations to Ancillary Operations

If a CIRA provides ancillary operations to its residents (and perhaps the public), then it should certainly consider separately accounting for these activities, perhaps set up as a profit center. If so, it is likely that some of the administrative staff time of the CIRA will be spent on the administration of these operations. If this is the case, it may make sense to conduct a periodic allocation of some administrative costs to the ancillary operations. Doing so will give users of the CIRA's financial statements a better view of the real profitability of these operations.

Reserve Study Expenditures

Most CIRAs must pay for a periodic *reserve study*, which is a capital planning tool that provides guidance and a detailed analysis of community assets. The initial reserve study requires an on-site inspection and examination of a CIRA's reserve fund, which is needed to develop a prioritized schedule of capital improvement projects, as well as a reserve funding plan to pay for them over the next 30 years. A less-detailed update to this study is conducted every three to five years, to assist a CIRA in maintaining an accurate forecast of future expenditures, as well as to ensure that adequate reserve funds are set aside.

> **Note:** Some states require a more thorough analysis that includes periodic structural inspections and mandatory funding for structural repairs.

A conservative treatment of the cost of a reserve study is to charge it to expense as incurred, since it does not directly provide any value over subsequent periods.

Management Fees

If a CIRA outsources some of its work to a management company, then this firm will charge a standard fee for its services, usually on a monthly basis.

Timeshare Expenses

A timeshare association incurs the cost of housekeeping for all units, which is a substantial expense. This includes the cost of housekeeping labor, unit supplies, and laundry. It also operates a front desk and reservation system for the complex. This requires staffing by multiple personnel, and so can represent a considerable expense.

Security Expenses

Any type of CIRA may provide security services for its residents. If so, this includes the labor cost for security patrols and the operation of any gates.

Environmental Cleanup Expenses

The government can impose substantial environmental remediation costs on a CIRA. This can be the case even when the entity was only peripherally involved in the environmental damage. There are specific items for which a CIRA is more likely to be held accountable for environmental damage, such as lead-based paint, underground heating oil storage tanks, and underground gasoline storage tanks. Leaks in storage tanks can result in the surrounding soil being declared hazardous material, which is extremely expensive to remediate. In addition, a CIRA may incur extra costs for the ongoing disposal of hazardous substances, such as pesticides and paint solvents.

These expenses are nearly always charged to expense as incurred. An exception is for the cost of asbestos treatment or removal; these costs can be capitalized, even if the issue was found in an existing structure, or it was acquired with a known asbestos problem.

In general, a liability for an environmental obligation should be accrued if both of the following circumstances are present:

- It is probable that an asset has been impaired or a liability has been incurred. This is based on both of the following criteria:

    o An assertion has been made that the business bears responsibility for a past event; and
    o It is probable that the outcome of the assertion will be unfavorable to the business.

- The amount of the loss or a range of loss can be reasonably estimated.

It is recognized that the liability associated with environmental obligations can change dramatically over time, depending on the number and type of hazardous substances involved, the financial condition of other responsible parties, and other factors. Accordingly, the recorded liability associated with environmental obligations can change. Further, it may not be possible to initially estimate some components of the liability, which does not prevent other components of the liability from being recognized as soon as possible.

Once there is information available regarding the extent of an environmental obligation, a CIRA should record its best estimate of the liability. If it is not possible to create a best estimate, then at least a minimum estimate of the liability should be recorded. The estimate is refined as better information becomes available.

Accounting for Payroll

There are several types of journal entries that involve the recordation of compensation for a CIRA. The primary entry is for the initial recordation of a payroll. This entry records the gross wages earned by employees, as well as all withholdings from their pay, and any additional taxes owed by the entity. There may also be an accrued wages entry that is recorded at the end of each accounting period, and which is intended to record the amount of wages owed to employees but not yet paid. Each of these types of compensation is based on different source documents and requires separate calculations and journal entries.

There are also a number of other payroll-related journal entries that an accountant must deal with on a regular basis. They include:

- Manual paychecks
- Employee advances
- Accrued vacation pay
- Tax deposits

All of these journal entries are described in the following subsections.

Primary Payroll Journal Entry

The primary journal entry for payroll is the summary-level entry that is compiled from the payroll register, and which is recorded in either the payroll journal or the general ledger. This entry usually includes debits for the direct labor expense, wages, and the CIRA's portion of payroll taxes. There will also be credits to a number of other accounts, each one detailing the liability for payroll taxes that have not been paid, as well as for the amount of cash already paid to employees for their net pay. The basic entry (assuming no further breakdown of debits by individual profit center) appears in the following exhibit.

Recordation of Basic Payroll

	Debit	Credit
Compensation expense (expense)	xxx	
Payroll taxes expense (expense)	xxx	
Cash (asset)		xxx
Federal withholding taxes payable (liability)		xxx
Social security taxes payable (liability)		xxx
Medicare taxes payable (liability)		xxx
Federal unemployment taxes payable (liability)		xxx
State unemployment taxes payable (liability)		xxx
Garnishments payable (liability)		xxx

The reason for the payroll taxes expense line item in this journal entry is that the CIRA incurs the cost of matching the social security and Medicare amounts paid by employees, and directly incurs the cost of unemployment insurance. The employee-paid portions of the social security and Medicare taxes are not recorded as expenses; instead, they are liabilities for which the CIRA has an obligation to remit cash to the taxing government entity.

A key point with this journal entry is that the compensation expense contains employee gross pay, while the amount actually paid to employees through the cash account is their net pay. The difference between the two figures (which can be substantial) is the amount of deductions from their pay, such as payroll taxes and withholdings to pay for benefits.

There may be a number of additional employee deductions to include in this journal entry. For example, there may be deductions for 401(k) pension plans, health insurance, life insurance, vision insurance, and for the repayment of advances.

When the withheld taxes and CIRA portion of payroll taxes are paid on a later date, use the entry format in the following exhibit to reduce the balance in the cash account, and eliminate the balances in the liability accounts.

Recordation of Payroll Tax Payments

	Debit	Credit
Federal withholding taxes payable (liability)	xxx	
Social security taxes payable (liability)	xxx	
Medicare taxes payable (liability)	xxx	
Federal unemployment taxes payable (liability)	xxx	
State withholding taxes payable (liability)	xxx	
State unemployment taxes payable (liability)	xxx	
Garnishments payable (liability)	xxx	
Cash (asset)		xxx

Thus, when a CIRA initially deducts taxes and other items from an employee's pay, it incurs a liability to pay the taxes to a third party. This liability only disappears from its accounting records when it pays the related funds to the entity to which they are owed.

Accrued Wages

It is quite common to have some amount of unpaid wages at the end of an accounting period, so accrue this expense (if it is material). The accrual entry, as shown next, is simpler than the comprehensive payroll entry already shown, because all payroll taxes are typically clumped into a single expense account and offsetting liability account. After recording this entry, reverse it at the beginning of the following accounting period, and then record the actual payroll expense whenever it occurs.

Recordation of Accrued Wages

	Debit	Credit
Wages expense (expense)	xxx	
Accrued salaries and wages (liability)		xxx
Accrued payroll taxes (liability)		xxx

The information for the wage accrual entry is most easily derived from a spreadsheet that itemizes all employees to whom the calculation applies, the amount of unpaid time, and the standard pay rate for each person. It is not necessary to also calculate the cost of overtime hours earned during an accrual period if the amount of such hours is relatively small. A sample spreadsheet for calculating accrued wages appears in the following exhibit.

Sample Accrued Wages Calculation

Hourly Employees	Unpaid Days	Hourly Rate	Pay Accrual
Anthem, Jill	4	$40.00	$1,280
Bingley, Adam	4	38.25	1,224
Chesterton, Elvis	4	37.50	1,200
Davis, Ethel	4	43.00	1,376
Ellings, Humphrey	4	41.50	1,328
Fogarty, Miriam	4	26.00	832
		Total	$7,240

Manual Paycheck Entry

It is all too common to create a manual paycheck, either because an employee was short-paid in a prior payroll, or because the CIRA is laying off or firing an employee, and so is obligated to pay that person before the next regularly scheduled payroll. This check may be paid through the CIRA's accounts payable bank account, rather than its payroll account, so the accountant may need to make this entry through the accounts payable system.

EXAMPLE

Elder Care Estates lays off Mr. Jones. Elder Care owes Mr. Jones $5,000 of wages at the time of the layoff. The accountant calculates that she must withhold $382.50 from Mr. Jones' pay to cover the employee-paid portions of social security and Medicare taxes. Mr. Jones has claimed a large enough number of withholding allowances that there is no income tax with-holding. Thus, the accountant pays Mr. Jones $4,617.50. The journal entry used is:

	Debit	Credit
Wage expense (expense)	5,000	
Social security taxes payable (liability)		310.00
Medicare taxes payable (liability)		72.50
Cash (asset)		4,617.50

At the next regularly-scheduled payroll, the accountant records this payment as a notation in the payroll system, so that it will properly compile the correct amount of wages for Mr. Jones for his year-end Form W-2. In addition, the payroll system calculates that Elder Care must pay a matching amount of social security and Medicare taxes (though no unemployment taxes, since Mr. Jones already exceeded his wage cap for these taxes). Accordingly, an additional liability of $382.50 is recorded in the payroll journal entry for that payroll. Elder Care pays these matching amounts as part of its normal tax remittances associated with the payroll.

Employee Advances

When an employee asks for an advance, this is recorded as a current asset in the CIRA's balance sheet. There may not be a separate account in which to store advances, especially if employee advances are infrequent; possible asset accounts that can be used are:

- Employee advances (for high-volume situations)
- Other assets (probably sufficient for smaller entities that record few assets other than trade receivables and fixed assets)
- Other receivables (useful if management is tracking a number of different types of assets, and wants to segregate receivables in one account)

EXAMPLE

Frogmorton Estates issues a $1,000 advance to employee Wes Smith. The accountant issues advances regularly, and so uses a separate account in which to record advances. She records the transaction as:

	Debit	Credit
Other assets (asset)	1,000	
Cash (asset)		1,000

One week later, Mr. Smith pays back half the amount of the advance, which is recorded with this entry:

	Debit	Credit
Cash (asset)	500	
Other assets (asset)		500

No matter what method is later used to repay the CIRA – a check from the employee, or payroll deductions – the entry will be a credit to whichever asset account was used, until such time as the balance in the account has been paid off.

Accrued Vacation Pay

Accrued vacation pay is the amount of vacation time that an employee has earned as per a CIRA's employee benefit manual, but which he or she has not yet used. The calculation of accrued vacation pay for each employee is:

1. Calculate the amount of vacation time earned through the beginning of the accounting period. This should be a roll-forward balance from the preceding period.
2. Add the number of hours earned in the current accounting period.
3. Subtract the number of vacation hours used in the current period.
4. Multiply the ending number of accrued vacation hours by the employee's hourly wage to arrive at the correct accrual that should be on the CIRA's books.
5. If the amount already accrued for the employee from the preceding period is lower than the correct accrual, record the difference as an addition to the accrued liability. If the amount already accrued from the preceding period is higher than the correct accrual, record the difference as a reduction of the accrued liability.

A sample spreadsheet follows that uses the preceding steps, and which can be used to compile accrued vacation pay.

Sample Accrued Vacation Spreadsheet

Name	Vacation Roll-Forward Balance	+ New Hours Earned	- Hours Used	= Net Balance	× Hourly Pay	= Accrued Vacation $
Hilton, David	24.0	10	34.0	0.0	$35.00	$0.00
Idle, John	13.5	10	0.0	23.5	27.50	646.25
Jakes, Jill	120.0	10	80.0	50.0	43.50	2,175.00
Kilo, Steve	114.5	10	14.0	110.5	40.00	4,420.00
Linder, Alice	12.0	10	0.0	22.0	35.75	786.50
Mills, Jeffery	83.5	10	65.00	28.5	29.75	847.88
					Total	$8,875.63

It is not necessary to reverse the vacation pay accrual in each period if the decision is made to instead record just incremental changes in the accrual from month to month.

EXAMPLE

There is already an existing accrued balance of 40 hours of unused vacation time for Wes Smith on the books of Kent Estates. In the most recent month that has just ended, Mr. Smith accrued an additional five hours of vacation time (since he is entitled to 60 hours of accrued vacation time per year, and 60 ÷ 12 = five hours per month). He also used three hours of vacation time during the month. This means that, as of the end of the month, the accountant should have accrued a total of 42 hours of vacation time for him (calculated as 40 hours existing balance + 5 hours additional accrual − 3 hours used).

Mr. Smith is paid $30 per hour, so his total vacation accrual should be $1,260 (42 hours × $30/hour), so the accountant accrues an additional $60 of vacation liability.

What if a CIRA has a "use it or lose it" policy? This means that employees must use their vacation time by a certain date (such as the end of the year), and can only carry forward a small number of hours (if any) into the next year. One issue is that this policy may be illegal, since vacation is an earned benefit that cannot be taken away (which depends on state law). If this policy is considered to be legal, it is acceptable to reduce the accrual as of the date when employees are supposed to have used their accrued vacation, thereby reflecting the reduced liability to the CIRA as represented by the number of vacation hours that employees have lost.

What if an employee receives a pay raise? Then increase the amount of his entire vacation accrual by the incremental amount of the pay raise. This is because, if the employee were to leave the CIRA and be paid all of his unused vacation pay, he would be paid at his most recent rate of pay.

Tax Deposits

When an employer withholds taxes from employee pay, it must deposit these funds with the government at stated intervals. The journal entry for doing so is a debit to the tax liability account being paid and a credit to the cash account, which reduces the cash balance. The following exhibit shows the entry needed if a CIRA were to pay a state government for unemployment taxes.

Recordation of State Unemployment Tax Payment

	Debit	Credit
State unemployment taxes payable (liability)	1,000	
Cash (asset)		1,000

Accounting for Income Taxes

Before delving into the income taxes topic, we must clarify several concepts that are essential to understanding the related accounting. The concepts are:

- *Temporary differences*. A CIRA may record an asset or liability at one value for financial reporting purposes, while maintaining a separate record of a different value for tax purposes. The difference is caused by the tax recognition policies of taxing authorities, who may require the deferral or acceleration of certain items for tax reporting purposes. These differences are temporary, since the assets will eventually be recovered and the liabilities settled, at which point the differences will be terminated. A difference that results in a taxable amount in a later period is called a *taxable temporary difference*, while a difference that results in a deductible amount in a later period is called a *deductible temporary difference*. Examples of temporary differences are:
  - Revenues or gains that are taxable either prior to or after they are recognized in the financial statements. For example, an allowance for doubtful assessments may not be immediately tax deductible, but

instead must be deferred until specific assessments are declared bad debts.

- o Expenses or losses that are tax deductible either prior to or after they are recognized in the financial statements. For example, some fixed assets are tax deductible at once, but can only be recognized through long-term depreciation in the financial statements. As another example, organizational costs are charged to expense as incurred for financial reporting purposes, but are deferred and deducted in a later year for tax purposes.

EXAMPLE

In its most recent year of operations, Tenerife Estates earns $250,000. Table also has $30,000 of taxable temporary differences and $80,000 of deductible temporary differences. Based on this information, Tenerife's taxable income in the current year is calculated as:

$250,000 Profit - $30,000 Taxable temporary differences
+ $80,000 Deductible temporary differences

= $300,000 Taxable profit

- *Carrybacks and carryforwards.* A CIRA may find that it has more tax deductions or tax credits (from an operating loss) than it can use in the current year's tax return. If so, it has the option of offsetting these amounts against the taxable income or tax liabilities (respectively) of the tax returns in earlier periods, or in future periods. Carrying these amounts back to the tax returns of prior periods is always more valuable, since the entity can apply for a tax refund at once, and recognize a receivable for the amount of the refund. Thus, these excess tax deductions or tax credits are carried back first, with any remaining amounts being reserved for use in future periods. Carryforwards eventually expire, if not used within a certain number of years. A CIRA should recognize a receivable for the amount of taxes paid in prior years that are refundable due to a carryback. A deferred tax asset can be realized for a carryforward, but possibly with an offsetting valuation allowance that is based on the probability that some portion of the carryforward will not be realized.

EXAMPLE

Spastic Estates has created $100,000 of deferred tax assets through the diligent generation of losses for the past five years. Based on the CIRA's poor finances, management believes it is more likely than not that there will be inadequate profits (if any) against which the deferred tax assets can be offset. Accordingly, Spastic recognizes a valuation allowance in the amount of $100,000 that fully offsets the deferred tax assets.

- *Deferred tax liabilities and assets.* When there are temporary differences, the result can be deferred tax assets and deferred tax liabilities, which represent the change in taxes payable or refundable in future periods.

EXAMPLE

Uncanny Properties has recorded the following carrying amount and tax basis information for certain of its assets and liabilities:

(000s)	Carrying Amount	Tax Basis	Temporary Difference
Accounts receivable	$12,000	$12,250	-$250
Prepaid expenses	350	350	0
Inventory	8,000	8,400	-400
Fixed assets	17,300	14,900	2,400
Accounts payable	3,700	3,700	0
Totals	$41,350	$39,600	$1,750

In the table, Uncanny has included a reserve for bad debts in its accounts receivable figure and for obsolete inventory in its inventory number, neither of which are allowed for tax purposes. Also, the CIRA applied an accelerated form of depreciation to its fixed assets for tax purposes and straight-line depreciation for its financial reporting. These three items account for the total temporary difference between the carrying amount and tax basis of the items shown in the table.

All of these factors can result in complex calculations to arrive at the appropriate income tax information to recognize and report in the financial statements.

Accounting for Income Taxes

Despite the complexity inherent in income taxes, the essential accounting in this area is derived from the need to recognize just two items, which are:

- *Current year.* The recognition of a tax liability or tax asset, based on the estimated amount of income taxes payable or refundable for the current year.
- *Future years.* The recognition of a deferred tax liability or tax asset, based on the estimated effects in future years of carryforwards and temporary differences.

Based on the preceding points, the general accounting for income taxes is as follows:

+/-	Create a tax liability for estimated taxes payable, and/or create a tax asset for tax refunds, that relate to the current or prior years
+/-	Create a deferred tax liability for estimated future taxes payable, and/or create a deferred tax asset for estimated future tax refunds, that can be attributed to temporary differences and carryforwards
=	Total income tax expense in the period

Tax Positions

A *tax position* is a stance taken by a CIRA in its tax return that measures tax assets and liabilities, and which results in the permanent reduction or temporary deferral of income taxes. For example, a CIRA might take a tax position when deciding whether an assessment for a major repair should be classified as a capital contribution, or whether a sale of common property results in a capital gain or a return of capital.

When constructing the proper accounting for a tax position, the accountant follows these steps:

1. Evaluate whether the tax position taken has merit, based on the tax regulations.
2. If the tax position has merit, measure the amount that can be recognized in the financial statements.
3. Determine the probability and amount of settlement with the taxing authorities. Recognition should only be made when it is more likely than not (i.e., more than 50% probability) that the entity's tax position will be sustained once it has been examined by the governing tax authorities. This probability is based on the facts, circumstances, and information available at the reporting date.
4. Recognize the tax position, if warranted.

Tip: Given the large financial impact of some tax positions, it makes sense to obtain an outside opinion of a proposed position by a tax expert, and document the results of that review thoroughly. This is helpful not only if the position is reviewed by the taxing authorities, but also when it is reviewed by the CIRA's outside auditors.

EXAMPLE

Armadillo Properties takes a tax position on an issue and determines that the position qualifies for recognition, and so should be recognized. The following table shows the estimated possible outcomes of the tax position, along with their associated probabilities:

Possible Outcome	Probability of Occurrence	Cumulative Probability
$250,000	5%	5%
200,000	20%	25%
150,000	40%	65%
100,000	20%	85%
50,000	10%	95%
0	5%	100%

Since the benefit amount just beyond the 50% threshold level is $150,000, Armadillo should recognize a tax benefit of $150,000.

If a CIRA initially concludes that the probability of a tax position being sustained is less than 50%, it should not initially recognize the tax position. However, it can recognize the position at a later date if the probability increases to be in excess of 50%, or if the tax position is settled through interaction with the taxing authorities, or the statute of limitations keeps the taxing authorities from challenging the tax position. If a CIRA subsequently concludes that it will change a tax position previously taken, it should recognize the effect of the change in the period in which it alters its tax position. A change in tax position should be based on the evaluation of new information, rather than from a new evaluation of information that was available in an earlier reporting period.

EXAMPLE

Armadillo Properties takes a tax position under which it accelerates the depreciation of certain equipment well beyond the normally-allowed taxable rate, resulting in a deferred tax liability after three years of $120,000.

After three years, a tax court ruling convinces Armadillo management that its tax position is untenable. Consequently, the CIRA recognizes a tax liability for the $120,000 temporary difference. At its current 20% tax rate, this results in increased taxes of $24,000 and the elimination of the temporary difference.

A business may conclude that a tax position has been effectively settled following its examination by the relevant taxing authority. The assessment of whether such settlement has occurred depends upon consideration of *all* of the following conditions:

- The taxing authority has finalized its examination procedures, including all administrative reviews and appeals.
- The CIRA does not intend to appeal any part of its tax position or engage in litigation.
- The probability that the taxing authority would examine any aspect of the tax position is remote, based on its policy for reopening closed examinations and the facts and circumstances related to the tax position.

A CIRA should derecognize a tax position that it had previously recognized if the probability of the tax position being sustained drops below 50%, based on the most recent facts and circumstances.

If there is a change in the tax laws or tax rates, a CIRA cannot recognize alterations in its income tax liability in advance of the enactment of these laws and rates. Instead, it must wait until enactment has been completed, and can then recognize the changes on the enactment date.

Deferred Tax Expense

Deferred tax expense is the net change in the deferred tax liabilities and assets of a CIRA during a period of time. The amount of deferred taxes should be compiled for each tax-paying component of the entity that provides a consolidated tax return. Doing so requires that the CIRA complete the following steps:

1. Identify the existing temporary differences and carryforwards.
2. Determine the deferred tax liability amount for those temporary differences that are taxable, using the applicable tax rate.
3. Determine the deferred tax asset amount for those temporary differences that are deductible, as well as any operating loss carryforwards, using the applicable tax rate.
4. Determine the deferred tax asset amount for any carryforwards involving tax credits.
5. Create a valuation allowance for the deferred tax assets if there is a more than 50% probability that the CIRA will not realize some portion of these assets. Any changes to this allowance are to be recorded within income from continuing operations on the income statement. The need for a valuation allowance is especially likely if a CIRA has a history of letting various carryforwards expire unused, or it expects to incur losses in the next few years. A cumulative loss in recent years is a strong indicator that a valuation allowance is needed. A CIRA should consider its tax planning strategy when determining the amount of a valuation allowance.

Interest and Penalties

When there is a requirement in the tax law that interest be paid when income taxes are not fully paid, a CIRA should begin recognizing the amount of this interest expense as soon as the expense would be scheduled to begin accruing under the tax law.

If a CIRA takes a tax position that will incur penalties, it should recognize the related penalty expense as soon as it takes the position in a tax return. Whether penalties should be recognized may depend on management's judgment of whether a tax position exceeds the minimum statutory threshold required to avoid the payment of a penalty.

If a tax position is eventually sustained, reverse in the current period any related interest and penalties that had been accrued in previous periods under the expectation that the position would not be sustained.

Interfund Accounting

If a CIRA elects to use fund accounting to record transactions, it may occasionally pay from one fund for an expenditure that relates to a different fund. When this happens, the accountant creates a receivable for the paying fund and a payable for the fund that has incurred the obligation. For example, if the operating fund is used to pay for a new air conditioning unit, the accountant would create a receivable from the replacement fund to the operating fund. In this case, the replacement fund would also record the expense, as well as the payable to the operating fund.

> **Tip:** Document all interfund transactions, along with repayment terms, to establish whether a receivable/payable situation actually exists, or whether a permanent transfer between funds has taken place.

CIRA Financial Statements

A CIRA is usually required to issue a complete set of financial statements to its residents. In this section, we provide an overview of these statements, and provide examples of how several of them would look.

Overview

The financial statements prepared by a CIRA should be prepared using the accrual basis of accounting. The *accrual basis* is a method of recording accounting transactions for revenue when earned and expenses when incurred. This differs from the *modified accrual basis* used by many CIRAs, where assessment revenue is recorded on the accrual basis, but expenses are recorded when cash is paid (the cash basis of accounting). In the latter case, a CIRA will need to adjust any cash basis transactions to the accrual basis before its financial statements can be audited under the Generally Accepted Accounting Principles (GAAP) framework.

A CIRA may elect to present financial statements using *fund accounting*, where activities are clustered into groups (funds) based on their specific activities. In essence, a *fund* is an entity used to account for specific activities to which resources have been allocated. Given the structure of most CIRA operations, a fund accounting presentation is a good way to show how resources are being used. Under this approach, a CIRA will likely record the bulk of its activities within two funds, which are the operating fund and the reserve (or replacement) fund (which is used for significant repairs and replacements). If a CIRA engages in any ancillary activities, such operating a golf course, then it may tack on additional funds for these activities. In addition, it may set up a settlement proceeds fund (for insurance payouts and lawsuit settlements), a special assessments funds, capital improvements fund, and so forth.

Types of Financial Statements

A CIRA typically issues a set of financial statements that includes the following documents:

- *Statement of revenues and expenses.* This report shows all revenues earned and expenses incurred during the reporting period, as well as an excess of deficiency of revenues over expenses.
- *Statement of comprehensive income.* If a CIRA has other comprehensive income[3], then it should include this report. Other comprehensive income may also be combined into a single extended statement of revenues and expenses. If a CIRA does not have any investments in debt securities classified as available-for-sale, then it does not have to issue this report.
- *Balance sheet.* This report shows the aggregate amounts of assets, liabilities, and fund balances as of the end of the reporting period. Assets are presented in their order of liquidity (where the items most easily convertible into cash are listed first), while liabilities are presented in their order of maturity (where the items most immediately due for payment are listed first).
- *Statement of changes in fund balances.* This report shows the beginning and ending fund balances, as well as the activities that occurred in between. Possible reconciling items include the excess or deficiency of revenues over expenses, contributions or distributions of capital, and permanent transfers between funds.
- *Statement of cash flows.* This report summarizes all cash flows from operations, investing activities, financing activities, and the net change in cash during the reporting period. The types of cash flows that a CIRA is likely to experience are classified within the following areas:
  - *Cash flows from operations.* Cash inflows come from operating assessments, assessments for major repairs and replacements, investment income, other income, and litigation settlements. Cash outflows come from operating expenses, replacement expenses, interest expense, and taxes.
  - *Cash flows from investing activities.* Cash inflows come from the sale of property and the sale of investments. Cash outflows are for property and equipment, and investments.

---

[3] Other comprehensive income for a CIRA includes all changes in equity, other than investments by and distributions to owners. This usually means that other comprehensive income includes unrealized gains and losses on debt securities classified as available-for-sale, as well as any excess of revenues over expenses.

- o *Cash flows from financing activities.* Cash inflows come from borrowings, the issuance of stock, initial contributions, and interfund transfers. Cash outflows are for the repayment of borrowings, interfund transfers, and refunds of excess assessments.

- *Accompanying disclosures.* The basic set of financial statement disclosures is covered in the following section.

A sample statement of revenues and expenses appears in the following exhibit.

Eldritch Estates
Statement of Revenues and Expenses
For the Year Ended December 31, 20X1

	Operating Fund	Major Repair and Replacement Fund	Total
REVENUES			
Member assessments	$1,630,000		$1,630,000
Late fees	11,000		11,000
Transfer fees	47,000		47,000
Bank interest	5,000	$4,000	9,000
Total Revenues	1,693,000	4,000	1,697,000
EXPENSES			
Operating expenses:			
Landscape maintenance	228,000		228,000
Property repairs and maintenance	74,000		74,000
Insurance	68,000		68,000
Utilities	108,000		108,000
Street repairs and maintenance	10,000		10,000
General administration:			
Compensation	537,000		537,000
Employee benefits	42,000		42,000
Payroll taxes	39,000		39,000
Legal fees	69,000		69,000
Office supplies	26,000		26,000
Telephones	25,000		25,000
Depreciation	18,000		18,000
Janitorial	13,000		13,000

Bad debt expense	9,000		9,000
Bank charges	6,000		6,000
Payroll processing fee	5,000		5,000
Audit and tax preparation	5,000		5,000
Reserve study update	4,000		4,000
Major repairs and replacements:			
Street repairs		200,000	200,000
Landscape renovations		89,000	89,000
Other infrastructure		42,000	42,000
TOTAL EXPENSES	1,286,000	331,000	1,617,000
Excess of Revenues Over Expenses	$407,000	-$327,000	$80,000

A sample balance sheet appears in the following exhibit.

Eldritch Estates
Balance Sheet
As of December 31, 20X1

	Operating Fund	Major Repair and Replacement Fund	Total
ASSETS			
Current Assets:			
Cash and cash equivalents	$38,000	$8,000	$46,000
Certificates of deposit	1,500,000	3,000,000	4,500,000
Resident assessments receivable	72,000		72,000
Allowance for doubtful accounts	-27,000		-27,000
Interfund balances	-85,000	85,000	--
Prepaid insurance	30,000		30,000
Total Current Assets	1,528,000	3,093,000	4,621,000
Property and Equipment:			
Land	160,000		160,000
Buildings and improvements	538,000		538,000
Machinery and equipment	109,000		109,000
Vehicles	24,000		24,000
Improvements to land	21,000		21,000
Less: Accumulated depreciation	-312,000		-312,000
Total Property and Equipment	540,000		540,000
TOTAL ASSETS	$2,068,000	$3,093,000	$5,161,000
LIABILITIES AND FUND BALANCE			
Liabilities:			
Accounts payable	$218,000		$218,000
Prepaid assessments	161,000		161,000
Total Liabilities	379,000		379,000
Fund Balance	2,447,000	3,093,000	5,540,000
TOTAL LIABILITIES AND FUND BALANCE	$2,068,000	$3,093,000	$5,161,000

A sample statement of cash flows appears in the following exhibit.

Eldritch Estates
Statement of Cash Flows
For the Year Ended December 31, 20X1

	Operating Fund	Major Repair and Replacement Fund	Total
CASH FLOW FROM OPERATING ACTIVITIES			
Excess of revenues over expenses	$407,000	-$327,000	$80,000
Adjustments to reconcile to net cash:			
Depreciation	18,000		18,000
(Increase) decrease in:			
Accounts receivable	46,000		46,000
Prepaid insurance	-1,000		-1,000
Increase (decrease) in:			
Accounts payable	-18,000		-18,000
Prepaid assessments	7,000		7,000
NET CASH PROVIDED BY OPERATING ACTIVITIES	459,000	-327,000	132,000
CASH FLOWS FROM INVESTING ACTIVITIES			
Purchase of certificates of deposit	-178,000	-211,000	-389,000
NET CASH USED BY INVESTING ACTIVITIES	-178,000	-211,000	-389,000
CASH FLOWS FROM FINANCING ACTIVITIES			
Transfers between funds	-247,000	247,000	0
NET CASH PROVIDED (USED) BY FINANCING ACTIVITIES	-247,000	247,000	0
NET INCREASE (DECREASE) IN CASH	34,000	-291,000	-257,000
CASH AT BEGINNING OF YEAR	4,000	299,000	303,000
CASH AT END OF YEAR	$38,000	$8,000	$46,000

Presentation and Disclosure Topics

This section contains the decidedly voluminous financial statement presentation and disclosure requirements for CIRAs, with separate treatment of common interest realty associations and cooperative housing associations.

Common Interest Realty Association Presentation Requirements

A full set of financial statements for a common interest realty association should include the following:

- Balance sheet
- Statement of revenues and expenses
- Statement of changes in fund balances or statement of changes in members' equity
- Statement of cash flows
- Accompanying notes to the financial statements

The statement of revenues and expenses should present information about an association's assessments, other revenues, and operational expenses. All activities other than the major repairs and replacement fund should be reported in this statement.

Depreciation expense is reported within the fund in which the related asset is reported.

The statement of changes in fund balances reconciles the beginning and ending balance in each fund. Reconciling items relate to the activities occurring within each reporting period including inter-fund receivables and payables. If there is a transfer between funds, this is presented as an inter-fund transfer, and not as revenue to the receiving fund.

EXAMPLE

The directors of the Willow Creek Association note that there are $50,000 of excess operating funds as of the end of the last year of operations, and decide to transfer it to the association's major repairs and replacements fund. In the statement of changes for the replacement fund, the incoming funds appear as a transfer, not as revenue.

Reported revenue should be broken down into categories to clarify sources, such as:

- Assessments charged to the developer
- Developer contributions and subsidies
- Interest income
- Lawsuit settlements
- Special-use charges
- Vending income

These classifications can be combined if they are not material. Interest income should be associated with a specific fund, unless the association has a policy for presenting it in a different manner.

When a CIRA issues periodic assessments to owners for future major repairs and replacements, it must present these amounts separately in its balance sheet from the amounts it assesses owners for normal operations. If fund reporting is used, these major assessments are to be reported in a fund that is separate from the operating fund. If an association also conducts commercial operations, these activities can be reported in separate funds.

When an association reports about an operating fund, it should provide several types of information to give the reader a full understanding of the status of the fund. This information should include the cash balance, assessments receivable, prepaid expenses, and accounts payable, as well as any property and equipment that have been reported as assets.

When an association reports about a major repairs and replacements fund, it should provide detailed information about all assets held for future replacement funding, such as cash, marketable securities, and short-term investments, as well as liabilities.

Common Interest Realty Association Disclosures

When a common interest realty association releases its financial statements, they should be accompanied by the following disclosures:

- The legal form of the entity (usually a corporation or association)
- The legal form of the entity for which the association provides services (such as a condominium or cooperative)
- The areas controlled by the association and the number of units (a coop may instead disclose the number of shares, while a time-share association may disclose the number of weeks)
- The services provided by the association (such as facility maintenance)
- Any subsidies provided by the developer
- The number of units, coop shares, or time-share weeks owned by the developer
- The proposed use of funds collected via special assessments
- The purposes to which assessments were put when the use differed from their original designation
- The funding for future major repairs and replacements, which includes the following information:
  - Any requirements to accumulate funds, and the association's compliance with those requirements
  - The association's funding policy (if any), and its compliance with that policy
  - The amounts assessed in the current period for major repairs and replacements
  - If a special assessment or borrowing was used to fund future major repairs and replacements, disclose this information
  - A statement that funds are being accumulated based on current or projected costs, that actual expenditures may vary from these estimates, and that there may be material variances from expectations

    o   A statement noting whether a study was completed to estimate the remaining useful lives of common property and the costs of future major repairs and replacements

For example:

Nature of Organization

Eldritch Estates was chartered under the laws of the State of Colorado on January 2, 20X1, as a corporation. The primary purpose of this corporation is to maintain and administer the common facilities and to collect and disburse the assessments and charges of the Association. The Association is located in Next Door, Colorado, and currently consists of 2,000 member lots on 1,300 acres.

Fund Accounting

The Association's governing documents provide certain guidelines for governing its financial activities. To ensure observance of limitations and restrictions on the use of financial resources, financial resources are classified for accounting and reporting purposes into an operating fund and a major repairs and replacement fund. The operating fund is used to account for financial resources available for the general operations of the Association. The major repairs and replacement fund is used to accumulate financial resources designated for major repairs and replacement of common elements available for use by all members of the Association.

Member Assessments

Association members are subject to monthly assessments to provide funds for the Association's operating expenses and major repairs and replacements. Assessment revenue is recognized as the related performance obligations are satisfied at transaction amounts expected to be collected. The Association's performance obligations related to operating assessments are satisfied over the period of assessment on a monthly pro-rata basis. The performance obligations related to special assessments for specific repairs are satisfied when these funds are expended for their designated purpose.

- The association's income tax filing status and income tax liability
- Any credits from taxation authorities that will be phased out in future periods

For example:

Income Taxes

The Association qualifies as a tax-exempt association for all income and expenses related to its exempt function purpose. The net non-exempt income from earned interest and nonmember fees is taxed at 21% or 30% by the federal government, dependent upon certain filing elections made. The Association can also elect to file as a regular corporation if it is in their best interest.

An association should also disclose the following unaudited information:

- Estimates of current or future major repairs and replacements, including the following information:
  - The methods used to determine costs
  - The basis for calculations (such as the interest rates and inflation rates used)
  - The sources used
  - The dates of the studies conducted

- The components to be repaired or replaced, their estimated remaining useful lives and replacement costs, and the funds accumulated for each one

Note: It is especially important to disclose information about current or future major repairs and replacements, since this information is critical to someone evaluating the amount of future assessments likely to be charged to residents.

For example:

Future Major Repairs and Replacements

The Association's governing documents require that the Association establish adequate reserve funds for major repair and replacement of Common Area components. This reserve is to be funded by regular assessments. Accumulated funds should be accounted for in separate certificates of deposit and savings accounts.

A study was performed by International Reserve Consultants during 20X1 to estimate the remaining useful lives and replacement costs of the components of common property. Because funding is based on estimates, actual expenditures may vary from the estimated future expenditures and the variations may be material. Monies accumulated in the replacement fund may not be adequate to meet all future needs for major repairs and replacements. Thus, the Board has the right to raise regular assessments or levy a special assessment to meet these needs.

Replacement costs from authoritative literature were based on estimated costs to repair or replace common property components at the replacement date using a projected inflation factor. The estimates in the following table were obtained from the reserve study and estimates may vary significantly from actual costs. The following table presents information about the components of common property.

	Estimated Remaining Useful Lives (years)	Estimated Current Replacement Costs	Components of Fund Balance
Asphalt pavement	0	$8,612,000	
Concrete flatwork	2 – 29	473,000	
Metal fences	1 – 29	902,000	
Irrigation system	8 – 29	429,000	
Landscape replacements	0	2,340,000	
Light fixtures	3 – 29	308,000	
Perimeter walls	2 – 11	635,000	
Retaining walls	5 – 11	181,000	
Trucks and street sweeper	2	351,000	
Air handling and condensing units	3 – 9	85,000	
HOA office	8 - 18	302,000	
		$14,618,000	$3,093,000
Reserve study ideal balance at year-end			$3,050,000
Percent of ideal balance on hand			101%

The following information should be disclosed about common property:

- The association's policy for recognizing and measuring common property
- A description of the common property recognized by the association in its balance sheet
- A description of any common property not recognized by the association in its balance sheet, but to which it has title or other evidence of ownership
- A statement regarding the association's responsibility to preserve and maintain the common property
- The terms and conditions associated with existing leases
- Any restrictions on the use of common property, or on how it can be dispositioned
- The depreciation expense for the reporting period
- The ending balances and accumulated depreciation in the major classes of depreciable assets
- A description of the methods used to calculate depreciation for the major classes of depreciable assets

For example:

Property Equipment and Depreciation

The Association recognizes real and personal property assets at cost to which it is entitled and may directly derive income. The property is depreciated over its estimated useful life using the straight-line method of depreciation. The following estimated useful life and depreciation expense are as follows:

Fixed Assets	Useful Life (Years)	Depreciation
Buildings and improvements	39	$14,000
Vehicles	5	4,000
		$18,000

Land is not depreciated.

Further, an association should disclose the proposed use of funds that have been collected through special assessments, as well as assessments used for alternative purposes than their original designations.

If at least 10% of the revenues of an association are derived from any one source (such as a developer or other third party), disclose the amount of revenue from each source.

It is possible that related parties are providing an association with insurance, maintenance assistance, or management services. In general, any related party transaction should be disclosed that would impact the decision making of the users of an association's financial statements. This involves the following disclosures:

- *General.* Disclose all material related party transactions, including the nature of the relationship, the nature of the transactions, the dollar amounts of the transactions, the amounts due to or from related parties and the settlement terms.
- *Control relationship.* Disclose the nature of any control relationship where the association and other entities are under common ownership or management control, and this control could yield results different from what would be the case if the other entities were not under similar control, even if there are no transactions between the businesses.
- *Receivables.* Separately disclose any receivables from officers, employees, or affiliated entities.

Depending on the transactions, it may be acceptable to aggregate some related party information by type of transaction. Also, it may be necessary to disclose the name of a related party, if doing so is required to understand the relationship.

When disclosing related party information, do not state or imply that the transactions were on an arm's-length basis, unless the claim can be substantiated.

Cooperative Housing Association Presentation Requirements

A full set of financial statements for a cooperative housing association is somewhat different from the requirement for the basic common interest realty association. The statements for a cooperative entity should include the following:

- Balance sheet
- Statement of operations
- Statement of changes in shareholders' equity
- Statement of cash flows
- Accompanying notes to the financial statements

The reported revenues for a cooperative should inform the reader about all charges to residents and other income. If there is activity in the paid-in capital account, a cooperative should also prepare a statement of shareholders' equity.

Cooperative Housing Corporation Disclosures

A cooperative should include in its disclosures a discussion of its funding policy (if any) for future major repairs and replacements.

A cooperative should not disclose the components of its retained earnings, nor should it allocate a portion of its retained earnings to an amount equal to accumulated depreciation.

Applicable Controls

There are many controls that a CIRA can implement to ensure that it is properly reporting financial information, and to keep it from losing assets. Here are some of the most important controls to consider installing:

Cash Controls

- Use a bank lockbox to accept all inbound payments.
- Reconcile cash receipts to the accountant's general ledger postings each day.
- Reconcile the bank statement on at least a monthly basis.

Investment Controls

- Verify that all investments have been classified correctly as either trading, available for sale, or held to maturity.
- Periodically verify that all investments follow the investment policy.
- Verify that all interest and dividend income is being recorded correctly.
- Reconcile investment statements to the general ledger.

Billing Controls

- Review all prospective billings for accuracy before they are issued.

Receivables Controls

- Review delinquent assessments receivable on a regular basis, and take action as necessary.
- File liens on unpaid assessments, as necessary.
- Approve all credit memos issued.
- Prepare a supporting analysis for the balance in the allowance for doubtful accounts.

Fixed Asset Controls

- Verify that all fixed assets exist and are on the premises.
- Verify that all depreciation calculations incorporate the correct useful life and depreciation method.
- Authorize all property disposals prior to the event.
- Periodically examine fixed assets for impairment and write down their cost as necessary.

Purchasing Controls

- Mandate management purchase order approval for all purchases over a threshold amount.
- Restrict access to the vendor master file, especially in regard to vendor remittance information.

Payables Controls

- Verify that supplier invoices were logged into the correct reporting period.
- Issue payments only after a review of the associated purchase order and receiving documentation.
- Checks are numerically controlled and stored in a locked location.
- Check signers review supporting documentation prior to signing checks.

Other Liabilities Controls

- Verify the formulation of all accrued liabilities.
- Use a checklist to ensure that a standard set of liabilities is accrued for in each period.
- Maintain supporting detail that itemizes all deferred revenue liabilities.
- Reconcile loan statements to the general ledger.

Equity Controls

- Perform an annual equity rollforward, and investigate any unusual items.

Payroll Controls

- Restrict access to the employee master file, especially in regard to compensation information.
- Run a payroll change log to spot any changes made to payroll information.
- Review and approve the preliminary payroll register, prior to finalizing the payroll.
- Review payroll results on a trend line to spot and investigate anomalies.

Fund Controls

- Verify that repair and replacement expenditures, as well as capital improvement expenditures, are recorded within the correct funds.

Financial Statement Controls

- A knowledgeable member of management reviews the financial statements before they are released.
- Management investigates significant financial statement variances from the budget.

General Controls

- There is adequate separation of duties. Ideally, no one person should initiate a transaction, approve it, record it, reconcile the transaction, and handle the related asset.
- Management periodically reviews the system of controls. This may involve an analysis by an outside controls expert.

Summary

The accounting for and reporting of transactions for a homeowners' association, as well as other common interest realty associations, is quite extensive. In this course, we have attempted to cover all areas of significance, including assessments, fixed assets, interfund accounting, and controls. If topics were not covered, that is because they were considered too generic, and so can be reviewed elsewhere, such as in the author's *Bookkeeping Guidebook* course.

Glossary

A

Accrual basis. A method of recording accounting transactions for revenue when earned and expenses when incurred.

Allowance for doubtful accounts. A reserve that represents management's best estimate of the amount of accounts receivable that will not be paid by customers.

C

Common interest realty association. An association of owners that is responsible for the provision of services and the maintenance of property that is shared by or owned in common by the owners.

Contra account. An account that offsets the balance in another, related account with which it is paired.

D

Deductible temporary difference. A difference between financial and tax records that results in a deductible amount in a later period.

Deferred tax expense. The net change in the deferred tax liabilities and assets of a CIRA during a period of time.

F

Fair value. The price that two parties are willing to pay for an asset or liability, preferably in an active market.

Finance lease. A lease in which it is implied that the lessee has purchased the underlying asset (even though this may not actually be the case).

Fund. An entity used to account for specific activities to which resources have been allocated.

Fund accounting. A method of recording accounting transactions where activities are clustered into groups (funds) based on their specific activities.

G

GAAP. Generally accepted accounting principles.

M

Modified accrual basis. A method of recording accounting transactions where assessment revenue is recorded on the accrual basis, but expenses are recorded when cash is paid.

O

Operating lease. A lease in which it is implied that the lessee has obtained the use of the underlying asset for only a period of time.

Other comprehensive income. A reporting classification that contains all changes that are not permitted to be included in profit or loss.

R

Reserve study. A capital planning tool that provides guidance and a detailed analysis of community assets.

T

Tax position. A stance taken by a CIRA in its tax return that measures tax assets and liabilities, and which results in the permanent reduction or temporary deferral of income taxes.

Taxable temporary difference. A difference between financial and tax records that results in a taxable amount in a later period.

Index